NO N(

MICROWAVE DIET COOKING

OTHER NO NONSENSE COOKING GUIDES

Cookies for Holidays & Every Day
Entertaining at Home
Appetizers, Hors d'Oeuvres & Salads
Breakfasts & Brunches
Fabulous Desserts: Mainly Microwave
Microwave Vegetable Dishes & Snacks
Microwave Main Courses, Quick & Easy

OTHER NO NONSENSE GUIDES

Real Estate Guides
Financial Guides
Business Guides
Legal Guides
Wine Guides
Home Repair Guides
Health Guides
Success Guides

NO NONSENSE COOKING GUIDE

MICROWAVE DIET COOKING

IRENA CHALMERS

LONGMEADOW PRESS

MICROWAVE DIET COOKING

Published by Longmeadow Press, 201 High Ridge Road, Stamford, Connecticut 06904.

ISBN 0-681-40276-8

Printed in the United States of America

0 9 8 7 6 5 4 3 2 1

STAFF FOR NO NONSENSE COOKING GUIDES

EDITORIAL DIRECTION: **Jean Atcheson**

MANAGING EDITOR: **Mary Goodbody**

COVER DESIGN: **Karen Skelton**

ART DIRECTION & DESIGN: **Helene Berinsky**

RECIPE DEVELOPMENT: **Marilyn Schanze, Cynthia Salvino**
AMERICAN COOKING INSTITUTE, ST. JOSEPH, MICHIGAN

ASSISTANT EDITORS: **Mary Dauman, Dorothy Atcheson**

PROJECT MANAGER: **Nancy Kipper**

COVER PHOTOGRAPH: **Gerald Zanetti**

TYPESETTING: **ComCom, Allentown, Pennsylvania**

PRODUCTION SERVICES: **William S. Konecky Associates, New York**

CONTENTS

MICROWAVE DIET COOKING

Using the microwave to prepare foods while you are dieting makes excellent sense for all sorts of reasons. First, food cooks quickly so that you can be in and out of the kitchen in record time—before any tidbits in the refrigerator have time to tempt you. Second, you can cook many foods without adding fats such as oil or butter, which you might have to use for cooking on top of a conventional stove. Third, it is no problem to cook small quantities in the microwave, which means you can quickly and efficiently prepare your own special low-calorie meals separately from the food other members of the household are eating.

All the foods that we *know* we should eat when dieting are ideal for the microwave. Fish, which is low in calories and fat and high in vitamins, is perfectly suited for microwave cooking. It cooks gently and evenly without becoming dry. Skinned chicken, equally good for everyone watching their weight, also does beautifully in the microwave.

And, of course, nothing beats the microwave when it comes to cooking vegetables. Many of them require no added liquid for microwave cooking, so their full flavor, color and vitamin content remain where they belong: within the vegetable. They retain their shape and texture during the short cooking time, too. If you want to cook a box of frozen vegetables, remove the outside wrapping, puncture the package a few times with a fork and put it in the microwave. The vegetables will defrost and then cook through in a matter of minutes—still in the container.

Every dieter needs a treat now and then, and one of the best ways to indulge when counting calories is to prepare a fruit dessert. As the recipes in this book demonstrate, microwaving is a wonderful way to cook fruit. Like vegetables, most fruits have a high water content and cook quickly and evenly with little loss of texture, shape, juiciness or flavor.

Even with the help of a microwave, though, a diet can be difficult. If you follow a few simple rules of good nutrition and common sense, you will find your plan works and the pounds will start to disappear. When that happens, the diet becomes suddenly easier.

A few sensible tips will help ensure success.

- Incorporate exercise into your daily life. Begin slowly and carefully and always consult your doctor before beginning an exercise program. Perhaps you could walk up a flight of stairs you normally avoid, or park your car on the far side of the parking lot, or take a brisk morning walk to the corner for the newspaper. Gradually work up to more active exercise. Join an aerobics class or map out a walking route to travel with a friend on a regular basis.
- Eat three meals a day. Begin the day with a sensible breakfast that includes about 300 calories. Do not skip lunch or dinner and try to keep each meal's intake of calories about equal. Anyone who claims the only way to lose weight is by skipping meals is fooling him- or herself and probably is a classic

"binge-er" who will drop a few pounds and then put back those same pounds plus a few extra by overeating as a "reward for being good."

- Eat well-rounded meals that include foods from the primary food groups. While you need a little fat, no more than a tablespoon or two a day is necessary. Eat plenty of protein and vegetables, and do not skimp on grains, cereals and dairy products. Vary your menus to keep your interest level up.

Dieting is not punishment. On the contrary, it is something positive and good that you are doing for yourself—and with recipes such as the ones that follow you will find a diet can be both tasty *and* successful.

NOTE: This book is intended for people who are dieting in order to lose weight and are counting calories, so the calorie count per serving is shown at the head of each recipe. For dieting convenience, we have also included brief nutrition counts alongside the recipes, showing the number of grams per serving of protein, carbohydrate (carb.), fats, cholesterol (chol.) and sodium. Anyone who is following a specifically restricted diet may want to check these and adjust the recipes accordingly.

USING YOUR MICROWAVE

MICROWAVE POWER AND TIMING

Most microwaves run on 600 to 700 watts, although some of the smaller models are less powerful. The recipes in this book have been developed for microwaves within this range but if yours is less than 600 watts, you will need to extend slightly the cooking times given in recipes.

Microwave cooking is not an exact science, so you cannot depend on time alone to determine when the food is cooked. Open the oven door during cooking to check the food for doneness and adjust times and power settings accordingly, just as you would in a conventional oven.

Remember: The amount of power can also be affected by various factors, such as use of other electrical equipment on the same circuit or even utility company procedures.

The temperature, size and shape of the food will affect the timing, too. Food at room temperature cooks more quickly than food just taken from the refrigerator.

POWER SETTINGS

Most of today's microwave ovens offer variable power settings ranging from High (100 percent power) to Low (10 percent). The higher settings are most often used for cooking or reheating, while the low settings are designed for simmering, defrosting or keeping food warm. Throughout this book, we have indicated the power percentage necessary for every recipe.

EQUIPMENT

You do not need any special utensils for basic microwave cooking, although as you become more adventurous you may want to invest in some of the equipment specially designed for the microwave, such as browning dishes or racks.

You cannot use metal containers, most aluminum foil, or even plates with a metallic trim because microwaves cannot pass through metal. If you put metal in the microwave, the waves will bounce off the metal and "arc," which means they will spark and sizzle. In some modern ovens, however, lightweight aluminum foil may be used for shielding parts of the food that might otherwise overcook.

Heatproof glass plates and dishes are ideal, as are most ceramics, porcelain or pottery. Test any utensil you are unsure about before using it in the microwave.

TESTING FOR "MICROWAVABILITY"

Put the utensil in the oven along with a 1-cup glass measure filled with tap water. Microwave on High (100 percent power) for 1 minute. If the dish remains cool while the water in the measure becomes hot, the utensil is safe to use, or "microwavable." If the dish becomes hot, it is absorbing microwave energy and should not be used. (During cooking, the transfer of heat from food *can* make microwavable dishes hot, so be sure to have potholders handy.)

MICROWAVE COOKING TECHNIQUES

Small, uniformly shaped pieces or amounts of food will cook more quickly than large. Shield the thinner parts of unevenly shaped foods to prevent overcooking.

Stir or rearrange food once or twice during the cooking process to help it cook more evenly. Rotating foods in the oven will achieve the same result.

Remember: Standing time is often part of cooking. Some foods will not seem completely cooked when removed from the microwave but the standing time will complete the process.

Use paper towels and plates, transparent wrap and wax paper in the microwave according to the recipe instructions. Dry plain white paper towels prevent spattering and absorb moisture. Wax paper makes a loose cover to hold in heat.

When a tight cover is needed to hold in steam and tenderize and cook food more evenly, use a casserole lid or transparent wrap rolled back slightly at one edge to allow for venting. Be careful of escaping steam as you remove a cover.

CHAPTER 1

APPETIZERS AND SALADS

When you are dieting, you can still have a three-course meal—a salad or appetizer can really spark up lunch or dinner so that you do not feel the least bit deprived. Try the Lentil and Feta Salad or the Seafood Salad with Mustard Dressing as a fine beginning for a light dinner—both are low-fat dishes that make you forget you are even counting calories.

When you invite friends, it is good to serve several of the low-calorie dips and finger foods described in this chapter. The Spinach Dip, Peppery Cream Cheese Dip, Stuffed Mushrooms or Oriental Chicken Wings are just a few good party ideas that are made in the microwave.

Spinach Party Ryes

Makes 24 **40 calories each**

These little open-faced sandwiches of spinach, mushrooms, peppers and melted cheese are sure to be popular at your next party. Prepare the sandwiches well before the party and then pop them in the microwave just before serving time.

10-ounce package frozen chopped spinach
2 tablespoons water
4-ounce can mushrooms, drained and finely chopped
⅓ cup plain low-fat yogurt
¼ cup chopped scallion
¼ cup chopped green or red pepper
24 party-size rye bread slices
6 slices Swiss cheese, quartered

Put the frozen spinach in a 1-quart microwavable bowl. Add 2 tablespoons water and cover. Microwave on High (100 percent) for 4 minutes. Break the spinach apart and microwave again, covered, on High (100 percent) for 2 to 4 minutes, until heated through. Drain well.

Put the drained spinach, mushrooms, yogurt, scallion and peppers in a bowl and mix well.

Spread each bread slice with spinach mixture and top with a quartered cheese slice. Cover a microwavable rack or plate with a paper towel and arrange 8 bread slices on top in a circle. Microwave on Medium (50 percent) for 3 to 4 minutes, until the cheese is melted. Repeat with the remaining party ryes.

Or wash fresh spinach thoroughly to remove grit. Rinse under the cold tap and put into a large microwavable dish. Cover and microwave on High (100 percent) for 5 to 8 minutes, until wilted and reduced.

PROTEIN	2 gm
CARB.	3 gm
FATS	2 gm
CHOL.	5 mg
SODIUM	97 mg

Cauliflower Parmesan Pickups

Makes 15 to 18 | **50 calories each**

1 medium-sized head cauliflower
4 tablespoons diet margarine
¼ cup fresh bread crumbs
¼ cup grated parmesan cheese
2 teaspoons dried chives, crushed
1 teaspoon paprika

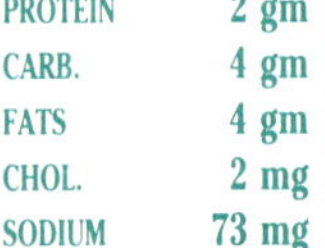

PROTEIN	2 gm
CARB.	4 gm
FATS	4 gm
CHOL.	2 mg
SODIUM	73 mg

Wash the cauliflower and pat it dry. Separate it into bite-sized florets.

Microwave the margarine on High (100 percent) for 30 seconds, until melted.

Combine the bread crumbs, cheese, chives and paprika in a plastic bag. Dip the cauliflower florets into the melted margarine, a few at a time, and drop into the crumb mixture. Shake the bag gently until the cauliflower florets are evenly coated. Repeat with the remaining florets.

Arrange 10 to 12 cauliflower florets around the outside edge of a 9-inch pie dish. Microwave, uncovered, on High (100 percent) for 2 to 3 minutes, until hot. Set aside and cover with foil to keep warm while you coat and heat the remaining cauliflower.

FETA FACTS

Feta cheese is available in many supermarkets and cheese shops in small, lidded tubs or in square packages, packed in brine, which keeps the low-fat cheese from drying out. Drain it and cover it with cold water to reduce the saltiness. It will keep this way for several days or longer, if well covered and refrigerated. Crumble it with your fingers, not a knife.

Lentil Salad with Feta Cheese

Serves 4 | 120 calories per serving

Using a microwave to soften dried lentils speeds the process considerably so that you can make this good-tasting salad very quickly.

½ cup dried lentils
2 cups water
1 bay leaf
¼ teaspoon dried thyme
1 teaspoon finely chopped garlic
⅛ teaspoon ground cloves
¼ cup chopped carrots
½ cup chopped celery
½ cup chopped red onion
¼ cup low-calorie Italian dressing
1 tablespoon red wine vinegar
2 teaspoons lemon juice
1½ ounces feta cheese, crumbled

Combine the lentils, water, bay leaf, thyme, garlic and cloves in a 2-quart microwavable dish. Cover and microwave on High (100 percent) for 5 to 7 minutes or until boiling.

Add the carrots, ¼ cup of celery and ¼ cup of onion and stir well. Cover and microwave on High (100 percent) for 10 to 14 minutes, until the lentils are tender, stirring every 4 to 5 minutes. Drain the lentils in a colander. Discard the bay leaf.

Put the warm lentils, salad dressing, vinegar and lemon juice in a serving bowl and mix well. Stir in the feta cheese and the remaining celery and red onion. Serve immediately or cover and refrigerate.

PROTEIN	6 gm
CARB.	15 gm
FATS	4 gm
CHOL.	10 mg
SODIUM	261 mg

Seafood Salad with Mustard Dressing

Serves 4 — **180 calories per serving**

Serve this salad on a bed of lettuce, or use it to fill tomato shells or zucchini boats.

1 tablespoon diet margarine
1 tablespoon all-purpose flour
1 tablespoon coarse-grained mustard
¼ teaspoon salt
¼ teaspoon paprika
1 cup evaporated skim milk, undiluted
6½-ounce can water-packed tuna
½ pound cooked shrimp
¾ cup peeled, seeded, chopped cucumber
¼ cup chopped celery
¼ cup chopped red onion
¾ cup chopped tomato
½ cup sliced mushrooms

Put the margarine in a 2-cup glass measure and microwave on High (100 percent) for 30 seconds, until melted.

Add the flour, mustard, salt and paprika and mix well. Slowly stir in the evaporated milk. Microwave, uncovered, on Medium (50 percent) for 5 to 6 minutes, stirring every 2 minutes, until the mixture just comes to the boil. Cover with transparent wrap and chill thoroughly.

Drain the tuna thoroughly and put in a large bowl. Add the shrimp, cucumber, celery, onion and tomato and mix well. Add the dressing and toss. Cover with transparent wrap and chill.

Stir in the mushrooms just before serving.

PROTEIN	22 gm
CARB.	13 gm
FATS	4 gm
CHOL.	78 mg
SODIUM	385 mg

Spinach Dip

Makes 3 cups (16 servings) **50 calories per serving**

This creamy spinach dip goes well with crackers or assorted fresh vegetables, such as cauliflower, broccoli, carrots, celery and cherry tomatoes.

2 slices bacon
10-ounce package frozen chopped spinach
2 tablespoons water
8-ounce package low-calorie cream cheese
¾ cup low-fat plain yogurt
8-ounce can water chestnuts, coarsely chopped
¼ cup chopped cucumber
1 tablespoon chopped chives or scallion greens
1 tablespoon lemon juice
1½ teaspoons beef bouillon granules
1 small clove garlic, finely chopped

Frozen spinach is always good to have on hand when you are planning a party—it blends well with many other flavors, is easy and quick to use and has very few calories.

Place the bacon on a microwavable rack. Cover with paper towel and microwave on High (100 percent) for 1½ to 2 minutes, until crisp. Drain on paper towels.

Remove the spinach from the package and place in a microwavable 1-quart dish. Sprinkle with 2 tablespoons of water. Cover and microwave on High (100 percent) for 5 to 6 minutes, gently breaking the spinach apart with a fork after 3 minutes. Drain thoroughly, pressing out excess moisture.

Put the cream cheese in a 4-cup glass measure. Microwave, uncovered, on High (100 percent) for 50 to 60 seconds or until softened. Stir in the yogurt, water chestnuts, cucumber, chives, lemon juice, bouillon and garlic. Mix well.

Crumble the bacon and stir into the cream cheese mixture. Add the spinach and stir well. Cover and refrigerate for 4 hours to give the flavors time to develop.

PROTEIN	2 gm
CARB.	4 gm
FATS	4 gm
CHOL.	11 mg
SODIUM	171 mg

Warm Spinach Salad

Serves 4 **110 calories per serving**

Spinach with a hot garlic dressing is a good first course.

3 tablespoons vegetable oil
1 clove garlic, finely chopped
¼ cup red wine vinegar
⅛ teaspoon salt
8 ounces fresh spinach, torn into bite-sized pieces
¼ cup slivered water chestnuts
¼ cup grated carrot

Put the oil and garlic in a 1-cup glass measure. Microwave, uncovered, on High (100 percent) for 30 to 45 seconds. Stir in the vinegar and salt. Microwave, uncovered, on High (100 percent) for 30 to 60 seconds, until boiling.

Pour the dressing over the spinach and toss until the leaves are well coated. Scatter the water chestnuts and grated carrot over the top and toss gently.

PROTEIN	2 gm
CARB.	5 gm
FATS	10 gm
CHOL.	0 mg
SODIUM	117 mg

Stuffed Mushrooms

Makes 25 to 30 **10 calories each**

Warm, generously stuffed mushrooms are usually among the first hors d'oeuvres to disappear at a party, and these will be no exception. You will need about one large potato to make the mashed potatoes.

1 pound large mushrooms
¾ cup mashed potato, made with skim milk
¼ cup low-fat cottage cheese

2 tablespoons dried onion soup mix
¼ cup chopped parsley

Wipe the mushrooms clean and carefully remove the stems. Finely chop the stems. Combine them with the mashed potato, cottage cheese, onion soup mix and 2 tablespoons of the parsley. Spoon the mixture evenly into the mushroom caps.

Arrange half the mushrooms in a circle around the outer edge of a microwavable 9-inch pie plate. Microwave, uncovered, on High (100 percent) for 2½ to 3½ minutes, until both mushrooms and filling are heated through. Repeat with the remaining mushrooms.

Sprinkle the stuffed mushrooms with the remaining parsley before serving.

PROTEIN	1 gm
CARB.	2 gm
FATS	0 gm
CHOL.	0 mg
SODIUM	112 mg

Peppery Cream Cheese Dip

Makes 1½ cups (8 servings) **100 calories per serving**

Serve this mildly spicy dip with a platter of assorted fresh vegetables, such as carrots, celery, zucchini, cauliflower, broccoli and cherry tomatoes.

8-ounce package low-calorie cream cheese
½ cup low-calorie mayonnaise
1 tablespoon dried onion
¼ teaspoon hot pepper sauce
½ teaspoon Worcestershire sauce
1 teaspoon chopped parsley

Put the cream cheese in a 1-quart microwavable casserole. Microwave on Medium (50 percent) for 1 to 2 minutes or until softened.

Stir in the onion, hot pepper sauce, Worcestershire sauce and parsley. Refrigerate before serving.

PROTEIN	2 gm
CARB.	2 gm
FATS	10 gm
CHOL.	20 mg
SODIUM	167 mg

Oriental Chicken Wings

Makes 15 to 18 | **170 calories each**

These gingery chicken wings are great "finger food."

1 tablespoon vegetable oil
1 tablespoon soy sauce
1¾ pounds chicken wings
1½ cups V-8 juice
1 tablespoon Worcestershire sauce
1 clove garlic, finely chopped
1½ teaspoons powdered ginger
1 tablespoon cornstarch
2 tablespoons water

Mix together the vegetable oil and the soy sauce and brush onto the chicken wings.

Arrange the wings around the outer edges of a rectangular microwavable baking dish. Microwave on High (100 percent) for 3 minutes. Turn the wings over and rotate the dish a half turn. Microwave on High (100 percent) for an additional 3 minutes. Drain the fat from the dish.

Combine the V-8 juice, Worcestershire sauce, garlic and ginger. Pour the mixture over the chicken wings. Cover the dish with transparent wrap and turn back at one corner to vent. Microwave on High (100 percent) for 5 minutes. Turn the wings over and rotate the dish a half turn after 3 minutes.

Remove the wrap and microwave on High (100 percent) for 8 minutes, turning the wings over and rotating the dish a half turn after 4 minutes.

Mix the cornstarch with the water to make a smooth paste. Stir the paste into the sauce in the pan. Microwave on High (100 percent) for 2 minutes, stirring every 30 seconds, until the sauce thickens. Pour the sauce into a small bowl and serve it as a dipping sauce or brush the wings with the sauce just before serving.

PROTEIN	22 gm
CARB.	4 gm
FATS	17 gm
CHOL.	67 mg
SODIUM	331 mg

CHAPTER 2

EGGS AND CHEESE

If two ingredients were "made" for the microwave, they are eggs and cheese. Scrambled eggs and omelettes cooked in the microwave are fluffy and light; crustless quiches and cheese sauces are beautifully smooth, and made almost in an instant. Soft cheeses such as Swiss and munster melt perfectly in the microwave and form velvety sheaths over the tops of sandwiches and casseroles.

Both eggs and cheese are excellent sources of protein. Eggs are low in calories and enormously versatile. When cooked in the microwave, they do not require any fat added to prevent them from sticking. Cheese is higher in calories than eggs, but a little added to a dish imparts the happy illusion that it is really every bit as rich as it tastes.

Country Omelette

Serves 4 | 140 calories per serving

A flavorful mixture of potatoes, peppers and onion gives the omelette a taste of the Mediterranean. It is easy to make an omelette in the microwave. Simply lift the edges with a spatula to let the uncooked egg run to the bottom of the pan.

1 tablespoon diet margarine
1 medium-size potato, peeled and diced
2 tablespoons chopped green pepper
⅓ cup finely chopped onion
1 tablespoon tomato ketchup
¼ teaspoon chili powder
4 large eggs, lightly beaten
Paprika

Put the margarine in a microwavable bowl and microwave on High (100 percent) for 30 seconds until melted.

Stir in the potato, green pepper, onion, ketchup and chili powder. Microwave on High (100 percent) for 4 to 5 minutes, stirring after 2 minutes. When they have softened, remove the bowl from the oven and set it aside while you prepare the omelette.

Spray a 9-inch glass pie dish with vegetable shortening spray. Pour the eggs into the dish and microwave on High (100 percent) for 1 minute. Lift up the cooked egg and allow the uncooked portion to flow underneath. Repeat this process twice, until the eggs are fully set.

Spread the warm potato mixture over one half of the omelette. Fold the other half over the top. Slide the omelette from the dish onto a serving platter. Sprinkle lightly with paprika before serving.

PROTEIN	8 gm
CARB.	10 gm
FATS	7 gm
CHOL.	252 mg
SODIUM	255 mg

Burrito Breakfast

Serves 2 **260 calories per serving**

Now that tortillas and salsa are available in nearly every supermarket, you can indulge in many Mexican-inspired dishes. Try this version of burritos first thing in the morning with a steaming cup of *cafe con leche* (strong coffee with hot milk).

2 large eggs
⅛ teaspoon black pepper
⅛ teaspoon cayenne pepper
2 large flour tortillas
¼ cup salsa
¼ cup chopped tomato
2 tablespoons sliced black olives
2 tablespoons grated sharp cheddar cheese
2 tablespoons plain low-fat yogurt

Beat the eggs with the black and cayenne pepper.

Spray an 8-inch glass pie dish with vegetable cooking spray. Pour the beaten eggs into the dish. Microwave on High (100 percent) for 3 to 4 minutes, lifting the egg after the first and second minutes to allow the uncooked portion to flow underneath.

Put the tortillas between 2 sheets of dampened paper towels. Microwave on High (100 percent) for 30 seconds.

Divide the cooked egg mixture between the tortillas. Top each with salsa, tomato, olives and grated cheese. Fold the tortillas over to enclose the filling. Spoon a tablespoon of yogurt over each tortilla before serving.

Flour (or wheat) tortillas are sold in many supermarkets. They tend to be a little larger than corn tortillas, but in most recipes calling for them, corn tortillas may be substituted.

PROTEIN	12 gm
CARB.	26 gm
FATS	12 gm
CHOL.	260 mg
SODIUM	375 mg

Western Scrambled Eggs

Serves 4 **160 calories per serving**

Scrambled eggs with peppers, scallions and cottage cheese turn this Sunday-morning favorite into a dish you could enjoy at any meal.

6 large eggs
¼ cup buttermilk
¾ cup low-fat (1 percent) cottage cheese
¼ cup diced scallion
¼ cup diced green pepper
¼ teaspoon salt
¼ teaspoon paprika

Put the eggs in a 1½-quart microwavable casserole and beat lightly. Stir in the buttermilk, cottage cheese, scallion, green pepper, salt and paprika.

Microwave on Medium (50 percent), stirring every 3 to 4 minutes, for 12 to 14 minutes or until the eggs are cooked to the desired consistency. Let the eggs sit for 1 to 2 minutes before serving.

PROTEIN	16 gm
CARB.	3 gm
FATS	9 gm
CHOL.	379 mg
SODIUM	423 mg

Two-Pepper Crustless Quiche

Serves 10 **120 calories per serving**

Jalapeño Monterey jack adds a slightly piquant flavor to this simple quiche. But you can also use plain jack.

1¾ cups low-fat (1 percent) cottage cheese
5 large eggs

3 large egg whites
¼ cup buttermilk
¼ cup all-purpose flour
1 teaspoon baking powder
¼ teaspoon salt
3 ounces mild jalapeño jack cheese, grated
¼ cup chopped green pepper
¼ cup chopped red pepper
Paprika

Put the cottage cheese in a food processor and process until smooth. Transfer to a large bowl.

Put the eggs, egg whites and buttermilk in the machine and process until light and fluffy. Add the flour, baking powder and salt. Blend until the mixture is smooth.

Stir the egg mixture into the cottage cheese and mix well. Stir in the grated cheese and the green and red peppers.

Spray an 8-by-11½-inch glass baking dish with vegetable shortening spray. Pour the egg mixture into the dish and microwave on High (100 percent) for 2 minutes and then rotate the dish a quarter turn. Microwave on High (100 percent) for another 2 minutes and rotate the dish another quarter turn.

Microwave on Medium (50 percent), rotating the dish a quarter turn every 4 minutes, for 10 to 12 minutes until a knife inserted near the middle of the quiche comes out clean.

Let the quiche stand for 3 to 4 minutes. Sprinkle lightly with paprika just before serving.

Never put unshelled eggs in the microwave—unless you have a dish specifically designed for this purpose—because they will explode. If you need hard-cooked eggs, cook them on a conventional stove.

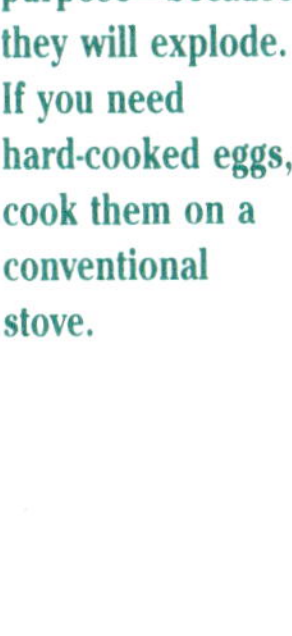

PROTEIN	12 gm
CARB.	4 gm
FATS	5 gm
CHOL.	136 mg
SODIUM	365 mg

Scalloped Potatoes

Serves 6 **110 calories per serving**

Scalloped potatoes—a creamy casserole of cheese and potatoes—may be a well-loved tradition in your family, but once you learn to make them in the microwave, you will want to serve them far more often since the cooking time is reduced to less than 15 minutes!

1 medium-size onion, thinly sliced
1 teaspoon diet margarine
½ cup skim milk
2 tablespoons grated parmesan cheese
1 tablespoon all-purpose flour
1 teaspoon salt
1 teaspoon instant chicken bouillon granules
¼ teaspoon ground black pepper
6 medium-size potatoes, peeled and sliced (about 4 cups)

Put the onion and margarine in an 8-by-8-inch microwavable dish. Microwave on High (100 percent) for 2 to 3 minutes, stirring after 1½ minutes, until the onions are softened.

Stir in the milk, cheese, flour, salt, bouillon and pepper. Put the potatoes in the dish and baste with the sauce. Cover the dish loosely with transparent wrap, turning back the corner to vent. Microwave on High (100 percent) for 10 to 14 minutes, stirring every 3 to 4 minutes, until the potatoes are tender. Allow to stand, covered, for 3 minutes before serving.

PROTEIN	4 gm
CARB.	21 gm
FATS	2 gm
CHOL.	4 mg
SODIUM	593 mg

Tuna Reubens

Makes 4 **190 calories per serving**

These substantial sandwiches are just right for a busy day when you want a filling lunch—but not a lot of calories. You can reduce its sodium content by using low-sodium tuna and cheese.

6½-ounce can water-packed tuna, drained
2 tablespoons low-calorie thousand-island salad dressing
4 slices rye bread, toasted
1 cup sauerkraut, drained
4 slices Swiss cheese

Combine the tuna and the dressing and spread a quarter of the mixture on each slice of toasted rye bread. Top each slice with ¼ cup of sauerkraut and a slice of cheese.

Place the bread slices on a microwavable rack or a folded paper towel. Microwave on Medium (50 percent) for 2½ to 3 minutes, until the cheese is melted.

PROTEIN	19 gm
CARB.	16 gm
FATS	5 gm
CHOL.	46 mg
SODIUM	1021 mg

CHAPTER 3

VEGETABLES

If you have heard nothing else about the convenience of microwaves, you have heard that they are "marvelous with vegetables." It's true. The microwave cooks all sorts of vegetables in very few minutes without the aid of pots of boiling water or steam. Color, flavor and nutrients remain where they belong—with the vegetable. For dieters, this is a special plus. It is possible to cook fresh broccoli or carrots or bake a potato in a flash, which means you are in and out of the kitchen quickly, carrying a plate full of low-fat, highly nutritious and superbly delicious vegetables before you are even tempted to nibble.

POTATO PLUSES

There is no need to forego potatoes just because you are dieting. A medium-size potato has only about 90 calories and when baked, it is very satisfying "as is" and needs no fat or oil. Four potatoes take 10 to 14 minutes to bake while two take just a little more than half the time.

Twice-Baked Potato

Serves 8 **60 calories per serving**

The microwave is a marvel for twice-baked potatoes. After the first baking, the centers are scooped out and the potato skins are filled with a creamy mixture of potato, scallions and cottage cheese and then sprinkled with paprika and heated through.

4 medium-size baking potatoes
1 cup low-fat (1 percent) cottage cheese
¼ cup skim milk
2 tablespoons chopped scallion tops or chives
Paprika

Scrub the potatoes in cold water and pierce each 2 or 3 times with a fork.

Arrange the potatoes in the microwave in a circle and microwave on High (100 percent) for 10 to 14 minutes until tender. Turn the potatoes over after 6 minutes of cooking.

Cut the potatoes in half lengthwise. Scoop out the centers with a spoon and save the skins for restuffing.

Place the potato in a bowl. Add the cottage cheese, milk and scallions and mix with a wire whisk or hand-held electric mixer set on medium speed until fluffy.

Spoon the mixture back into the potato skins. Arrange in a circle on a microwavable dish. Sprinkle with paprika and microwave on High (100 percent) for 4 to 5 minutes, until heated through.

PROTEIN	5 gm
CARB.	10 gm
FATS	0 gm
CHOL.	0 mg
SODIUM	118 mg

Vegetable Fruit Curry

Serves 4

210 calories per serving without rice
290 calories per serving with rice

Serve with rice and quickly grilled fish or chicken—larger portions for the non-dieters, of course.

1 tablespoon diet margarine
1 tablespoon vegetable oil
½ teaspoon ground ginger
2 teaspoons curry powder
1 teaspoon finely chopped garlic
1 cup fresh broccoli florets
1 cup fresh cauliflower florets
½ cup diced green pepper
1 cup sliced celery, cut on the diagonal
¼ cup chicken broth
8-ounce can mandarin orange sections, drained
8-ounce can pineapple chunks, drained
¼ cup raisins
2 tablespoons unsalted cashews
2 cups cooked rice (optional)

Put the margarine and the oil in a microwavable baking dish. Microwave on High (100 percent) for 30 to 40 seconds until the margarine is melted.

Add the ginger, curry powder and garlic and microwave on High (100 percent) for 30 seconds.

Add the broccoli, cauliflower, green pepper, and celery. Cover with transparent wrap, turning back one corner to let steam escape, and microwave on High (100 percent) for 2 to 4 minutes, until the vegetables are slightly tender. Remove the wrap, taking care not to burn yourself.

Add the chicken broth, stir well and cover again. Microwave on High (100 percent) for 3 to 4 minutes, until the vegetables are crisp-tender.

PROTEIN	4 gm
CARB.	29 gm
FATS	9 gm
CHOL.	0 mg
SODIUM	156 mg

Stir in the mandarin oranges, pineapple chunks, raisins and cashews. Cover and allow to stand for 2 minutes. Serve with rice.

Oriental Green Beans

Serves 4 **60 calories per serving**

This method of preparing frozen green beans is quick, easy and appealing. Serve them with chicken or pork, stir-fried with sweet red peppers.

10-ounce package frozen French-style green beans
¼ cup slivered water chestnuts
2 tablespoons water
2 teaspoons diet margarine
¼ cup chopped scallions
¼ pound mushrooms, sliced
1 tablespoon soy sauce

Put the green beans and mushrooms in a 1-quart microwavable dish. Sprinkle with the water, cover and microwave on High (100 percent) for 3 minutes, until the beans are thawed. Drain in a colander.

Put the margarine and scallions in the same dish and microwave on High (100 percent) for 1 minute to soften the scallions. Stir in the beans, water chestnuts, and soy sauce. Microwave, uncovered, on High for 3 to 4 minutes, until heated through.

PROTEIN	2 gm
CARB.	8 gm
FATS	2 gm
CHOL.	0 mg
SODIUM	397 mg

Spinach Stir-Fry

Serves 4 **60 calories per serving**

How can you stir-fry in a microwave? Easily, as this simple recipe demonstrates. Wash the spinach carefully to remove sand and grit.

1 tablespoon vegetable oil
1 cup sliced celery, cut on the diagonal
¼ cup sliced mushrooms
¼ cup chopped onion
1 tablespoon lemon juice
1¼ teaspoons soy sauce
1 teaspoon sugar
4 cups fresh, torn spinach leaves, well washed

Put the vegetable oil in a large microwavable bowl and microwave on High (100 percent) for 45 seconds. Add the celery, mushrooms and onion and mix well. Microwave on High (100 percent) for 1½ to 2 minutes, until slightly tender.

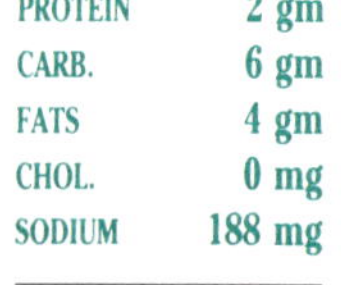

PROTEIN	2 gm
CARB.	6 gm
FATS	4 gm
CHOL.	0 mg
SODIUM	188 mg

Combine the lemon juice, soy sauce and sugar in a large bowl. Add the spinach and toss well.

Stir the spinach pieces into the soy mixture and toss well. Transfer the spinach to the cooked vegetables and mix thoroughly. Microwave on High (100 percent) for 1½ to 2 minutes, until the spinach is wilted.

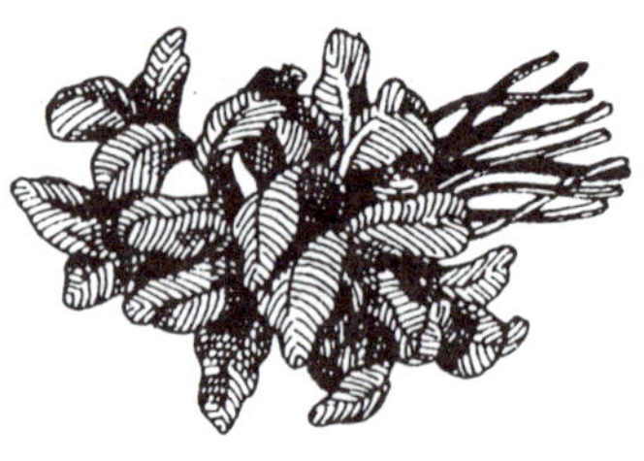

Broccoli and Pepper Pie

Serves 6 **80 calories per serving**

This pie-without-a-crust can be prepared in minutes the night before a family dinner or buffet. It can be refrigerated and then heated through in the microwave before serving.

1 cup chopped green pepper
½ cup chopped onion
1 small clove garlic, finely chopped
1 teaspoon olive or vegetable oil
10-ounce package frozen chopped broccoli, thawed and drained
¾ cup skim milk
3 large eggs
¼ teaspoon salt
1 teaspoon dried basil
⅛ teaspoon cayenne pepper

Put the green pepper, onion, garlic and olive oil in a 9-inch microwavable pie dish. Microwave, uncovered, on High (100 percent) for 1 to 2 minutes, until the vegetables have softened. Stir in the broccoli.

Beat together the milk, eggs, salt, basil and cayenne pepper. Pour the mixture over the vegetables.

Microwave on Medium (50 percent) for 16 to 18 minutes, rotating the dish a quarter turn every 4 minutes. Let the casserole stand for 5 minutes before serving to give the flavors time to blend.

PROTEIN	7 gm
CARB.	7 gm
FATS	4 gm
CHOL.	127 mg
SODIUM	155 mg

Brussels Sprouts in Lemon Mustard Sauce

Serves 4 | **60 calories per serving**

One bite of these tender brussels sprouts lightly coated with a lemon sauce will dispel any unpopular myths about the late autumn vegetable. We recomend fresh brussels sprouts.

1 pound brussels sprouts
2 tablespoons water
2 teaspoons diet margarine
1½ tablespoons lemon juice
1½ teaspoons coarse-grained mustard

Rinse the sprouts in cold water and, using a sharp paring knife, cut a ¼-inch-deep cross in the bottom of each.

Arrange the sprouts in a single layer in a 9-inch microwavable glass pie dish. Sprinkle with the water and cover with transparent wrap. Turn back one corner of the wrap to let the steam escape.

Microwave on High (100 percent) for 7 to 10 minutes, rotating the pie dish a quarter turn every 3 minutes. The sprouts should be barely tender.

Put the margarine in a 1-cup glass measure and microwave on High (100 percent) for 30 seconds until melted. Stir in the lemon juice and mustard.

Take care not to burn yourself as you remove the wrap from the pie dish holding the sprouts. Pour the sauce over the sprouts and toss gently to coat.

PROTEIN	3 gm
CARB.	10 gm
FATS	2 gm
CHOL.	0 mg
SODIUM	47 mg

Ravioli with Red Pepper and Tomato Sauce

Serves 4 | **190 calories per serving**

We suggest serving this red sauce, which is sweetened by juicy red peppers, over cheese ravioli, but it would be delicious with linguine or spaghetti as well.

1 small onion, chopped
1 clove garlic, finely chopped
1 tablespoon olive oil
2 medium-size red peppers, halved, seeded and cut into ½-inch pieces
1 cup drained canned whole tomatoes, crushed
½ cup tomato sauce
1 teaspoon dried oregano
¼ teaspoon crushed red pepper flakes
1 teaspoon sugar
12 ounces cheese ravioli

Put the onion, garlic and olive oil in a 2-quart microwavable casserole with a cover. Microwave on High (100 percent), uncovered, for 1½ to 2 minutes, until the onion softens.

Add the red peppers, cover and microwave on High (100 percent) for 2 minutes, stirring after 1 minute.

Add the tomatoes, tomato sauce, oregano and red pepper flakes. Cover, and microwave on High (100 percent) for 8 to 12 minutes until the peppers are tender, stirring after 4 minutes. Stir in the sugar.

Cook the ravioli according to the package directions. Drain well and turn into a serving bowl. Spoon the hot red pepper sauce over the top.

PROTEIN	5 gm
CARB.	20 gm
FATS	10 gm
CHOL.	43 mg
SODIUM	589 mg

Creamy Potato Casserole

Serves 8 **80 calories per serving**

Enrich a supper of simply broiled fish fillets and mixed green salad with these creamy, but low-calorie potatoes.

4 medium-size boiling potatoes, peeled and quartered
2 tablespoons water
1 cup plain low-fat yogurt
1 cup low-fat (1 percent) cottage cheese
¼ cup chopped scallion greens or chives
1 small clove garlic, finely chopped
Paprika

Put the potatoes in a microwavable loaf pan. Add the water. Cover with transparent wrap and microwave on High (100 percent) for 7 to 10 minutes, until softened. Remove the cover, taking care not to burn yourself as the steam is released.

Drain the potatoes and dice them. Mix with the yogurt, cottage cheese, scallion greens and garlic.

Spray an 8-by-8-inch microwavable pan with vegetable cooking spray. Spread the potato mixture evenly in the pan. Microwave, uncovered, on Medium (50 percent) for 6 to 8 minutes, until bubbling. Sprinkle with paprika before serving.

PROTEIN	5 gm
CARB.	11 gm
FATS	1 gm
CHOL.	4 mg
SODIUM	127 mg

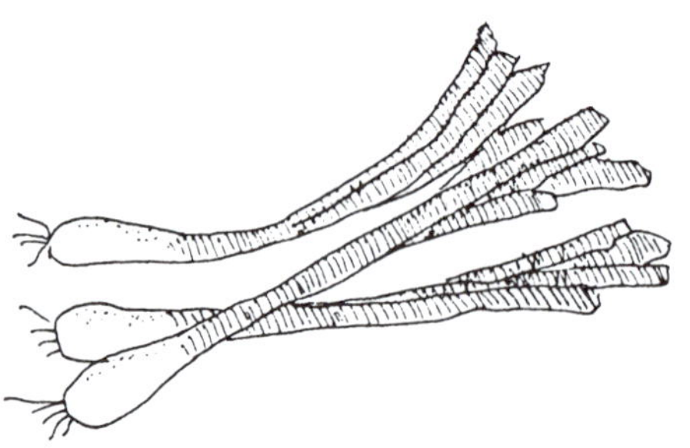

Squash and Apple Casserole

Serves 4 | 130 calories per serving

The microwave makes quick work of cooking butternut squash with apples and spices for a dish redolent with the full flavors of autumn.

1 medium-size butternut squash (about 1 pound)
1 tablespoon diet margarine
1 tablespoon lemon juice
2 Golden Delicious apples, cored and chopped
1 tablespoon white wine or dry vermouth
¼ teaspoon cinnamon
⅛ teaspoon ground cloves
1 teaspoon brown sugar
1 tablespoon chopped pecans

Scrub the squash and rinse well. Microwave on High (100 percent) for 2 minutes. Cut it in half and remove the seeds. Place the squash, hollow side up, in a microwavable baking dish. Cover with transparent wrap. Microwave on High (100 percent) for 10 to 12 minutes until tender, rotating the dish a half turn after 5 minutes. Let stand for 5 minutes.

Put the margarine and the lemon juice in an 8-by-8-inch microwavable dish. Microwave on High (100 percent) for 30 seconds, until melted.

Add the apples to the melted margarine and stir until well coated. Microwave, uncovered, on High (100 percent) for 1½ to 3 minutes, stirring after 45 seconds, until the apples are soft. Stir in the wine, cinnamon and cloves and microwave on High (100 percent) for 1 to 2 minutes, until hot.

Scoop the squash from its skin and mash well. Stir in the brown sugar.

Combine the mashed squash with the apple mixture. Transfer to a serving dish and sprinkle with the pecans.

PROTEIN	2 gm
CARB.	22 gm
FATS	5 gm
CHOL.	0 mg
SODIUM	37 mg

Sesame Asparagus

Serves 3 | **70 calories per serving**

Asparagus and sesame seeds are a fine combination of flavors.

1 pound thin, fresh asparagus, trimmed
2 tablespoons water
¼ teaspoon salt
1 tablespoon diet margarine
1 tablespoons sesame seeds, toasted

Lay the asparagus in a 1-quart microwavable casserole with a cover. Add the water, cover and microwave on High (100 percent) for 3 minutes, turning the casserole a half turn after 1½ minutes.

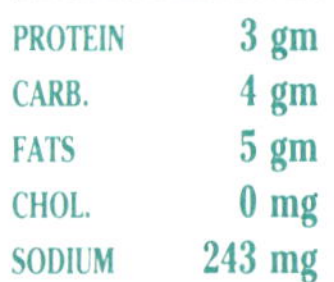

PROTEIN	3 gm
CARB.	4 gm
FATS	5 gm
CHOL.	0 mg
SODIUM	243 mg

Drain the asparagus. Gently rearrange the spears in the casserole. Sprinkle with salt and add the margarine. Cover and microwave on High (100 percent) for 3 to 4 minutes or until the asparagus is tender, redistributing the spears after 1½ minutes.

Sprinkle with sesame seeds just before serving.

TOASTING SESAME SEEDS

Toasting really brings out the flavor of sesame seeds. Spread the seeds out in a small frying pan and cook them over medium-high heat just until you can smell the aroma. Move the pan back and forth to prevent burning.

CHAPTER 4

SOUPS, STEWS AND CASSEROLES

Soups are a favorite with dieters. They are simple to make, use a variety of interesting low-calorie ingredients such as vegetables and broth, and are filling and satisfying. Plus, if you are cooking for your family, no one will look upon soup as a "diet" food. Serve it with hot biscuits or a loaf of bread (you can pass on these) and everyone will be happy.

Stews are, in some ways, a step or two beyond soup. They have a little less liquid and the ingredients are usually cut or chopped in larger pieces.

Soups, stews and casseroles all have the advantage of being cooked in one pot, very often the same pot from which they can be served at the table and in which any leftovers can conveniently be stored.

Be careful to use only ceramic, glass or plastic containers in the microwave.

Winter Vegetable Chowder

Makes 6 servings **130 calories per serving**

The list of ingredients is long because so many vegetables go into making this full-flavored, stew-like soup. Substitute your favorite vegetables for any listed here, but leave in the potatoes so that it remains an authentic chowder.

1 tablespoons diet margarine
½ cup chopped celery
1 cup chopped onion
2 cups water
1 large potato
2 medium-size carrots, thinly sliced
1½ teaspoons crushed, dried basil
1 beef bouillon cube
Salt and pepper
1 medium-size zucchini, halved and thinly sliced
7-ounce can whole-kernel corn, including liquid
1 tablespoon flour
⅔ cup evaporated skim milk, at room temperature
¼ cup grated cheddar cheese

Put the margarine in a 3-quart microwavable casserole and microwave on High (100 percent) for 30 seconds, until melted.

Stir in the celery and onion. Cover, and microwave on High (100 percent) for 2½ minutes, until tender.

Add the water, potato, carrots, basil, and pepper. Crumble in the bouillon cube. Cover, and microwave on High (100 percent) for 11 to 12 minutes, until the vegetables are just tender. Season to taste with salt and pepper.

Add the zucchini and the corn, cover, and microwave on High (100 percent) for 3 to 4 minutes.

Combine the flour with a little of the evaporated milk

PROTEIN	6 gm
CARB.	19 gm
FATS	4 gm
CHOL.	6 mg
SODIUM	349 mg

and stir until smooth. Stir in the remaining milk. Add this to the vegetable mixture. Microwave on High (100 percent) for 3 to 4 minutes, stirring every minute, until just boiling. Add the cheese and stir until melted.

Manhattan Clam Chowder

Serves 6 **145 calories per serving**

This is the clam chowder that uses tomatoes.

2 tablespoons diet margarine
1 cup finely chopped onion
¼ cup finely chopped carrot
¼ cup finely chopped celery
4 large tomatoes, peeled, seeded and chopped
1½ cups water
8 ounces tomato sauce
1 bay leaf
1 teaspoon dried thyme
¼ teaspoon black pepper
3 small potatoes, peeled and chopped
2 cups canned whole clams, including any liquor

Place the margarine in a 3-quart, microwavable casserole and microwave on High (100 percent) for 30 to 40 seconds, until melted.

Add the onion, carrot and celery. Cover, and microwave on High (100 percent) for 4 to 5 minutes, until the vegetables are tender.

Add the tomatoes, water, tomato sauce, bay leaf, thyme, pepper and potatoes. Cover, and microwave on High (100 percent) for 8 to 10 minutes.

Stir in the clams and any liquor and microwave on High (100 percent) for 2 to 3 minutes. Discard the bay leaf before serving.

PROTEIN	7 gm
CARB.	27 gm
FATS	6 gm
CHOL.	68 mg
SODIUM	723 mg

Fast Minestrone

Serves 4 **290 calories per serving**

You can have this vegetable soup cooked and ready to serve in about 20 minutes. To reduce its sodium content, use plain, unsauced lima beans and chopped fresh tomatoes.

¼ cup chopped onion
1 clove garlic, finely chopped
1 medium-size zucchini, sliced
1 tablespoon diet margarine
10-ounce package frozen lima beans in butter sauce
2½ cups beef broth
8-ounce can whole tomatoes, chopped and juices reserved
¾ cup broken pieces uncooked vermicelli
2 tablespoons grated parmesan cheese
¼ teaspoon pepper
½ teaspoon dried basil
½ teaspoon thyme
⅛ teaspoon cayenne pepper

Put the onion, garlic, zucchini and margarine in a 1½-quart microwavable casserole. Cover and microwave on High (100 percent) for 4 to 5 minutes, stirring after 2 minutes, until the onion is softened.

Remove the lima beans from the pouch and add them to the onion mixture. Stir in the beef broth, tomatoes, vermicelli, 1 tablespoon parmesan cheese, pepper, basil, thyme and cayenne pepper. Cover and microwave on High (100 percent) for 13 to 15 minutes, stirring every 5 minutes, until the vermicelli is tender.

Sprinkle with the remaining cheese before serving.

PROTEIN	18 gm
CARB.	43 gm
FATS	7 gm
CHOL.	4 mg
SODIUM	1036 mg

Hearty Turkey Soup

Serves 8 **290 calories per serving**

A sensational way to use up the last of the leftover turkey. Either dark or light meat may be used for the soup, though there is a little more flavor in dark meat.

1 cup chopped onion
2 cloves garlic, finely chopped
1 cup thinly sliced carrots
3 cups chicken broth
2 tablespoons flour
1 teaspoon salt
1 teaspoon dried marjoram or thyme, crushed
1/8 teaspoon ground black pepper
1/2 cup dry white wine or vermouth (optional)
15-ounce can tomatoes, chopped and juices reserved
10-ounce package frozen peas
2 1/2 cups cooked turkey, cut into small pieces

Place the onion and garlic in a 4-quart microwavable casserole. Cover and microwave on High (100 percent) for 2 minutes until tender.

Add the carrots and 1/2 cup broth. Cover and microwave on High (100 percent) for 5 minutes.

Blend in the flour, salt, marjoram, pepper, wine and the remaining 2 1/2 cups broth. Cover and microwave on High (100 percent) for 4 to 5 minutes.

Add the tomatoes and the reserved juice, peas and turkey to the casserole. Cover and microwave on High (100 percent) for 8 to 10 minutes, stirring after 4 minutes, until the vegetables are tender and the soup is hot.

PROTEIN	25 gm
CARB.	14 gm
FATS	13 gm
CHOL.	85 mg
SODIUM	868 mg

Lamb Stew with Indian Spices

Serves 4 | **230 calories per serving without rice**
310 calories per serving with rice

Middle Eastern and Indian cooks use herbs and spices far more freely than we do, which is what gives so many of their recipes exotic, mysterious flavors with layer upon layer of taste sensations. You can find all of the seasonings for this stew at the supermarket.

1 pound well-trimmed lean lamb, cut into cubes
1 cup plain low-fat yogurt
1 teaspoon ground coriander
1 teaspoon ground cumin
½ teaspoon cinnamon
½ teaspoon ground cardamom
½ teaspoon chili powder
¼ teaspoon ground cloves
½ teaspoon grated fresh ginger
1 onion, chopped
2 small cloves garlic, finely chopped
1 tablespoon olive oil
3 ripe tomatoes, peeled, seeded and chopped
1 teaspoon ground turmeric
⅓ cup water
½ teaspoon salt
3 cups hot cooked rice

Remove any fat from the lamb and put the cubes in a glass bowl. Add the yogurt, coriander, cumin, cinnamon, cardamom, chili powder, cloves and ginger and toss gently to combine. Cover and refrigerate for 6 to 8 hours, or overnight.

Combine the onion, garlic and olive oil in a 1½-quart microwavable casserole. Microwave on High (100 percent) for 1½ to 2 minutes, until the onion is softened.

Add the tomatoes and turmeric to the casserole. Microwave on High (100 percent) for 1 minute.

Add the meat and the marinade to the casserole. Stir in the water and the salt. Cover and microwave on Medium (50 percent) for 15 minutes, stirring every 5 minutes. Remove the cover and microwave on Medium (50 percent) for 8 to 10 minutes more, stirring after 4 minutes, until the lamb is tender. Serve over the hot cooked rice.

PROTEIN	15 gm
CARB.	7 gm
FATS	16 gm
CHOL.	59 mg
SODIUM	272 mg

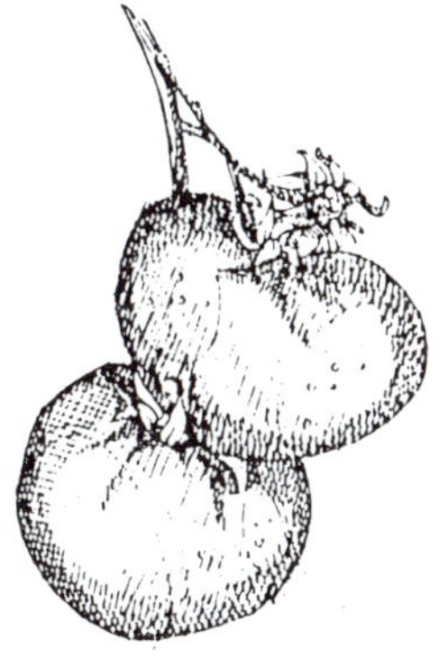

SEASONED SEASONING

Microwave cooking is so fast and efficient that it does not always allow flavors to mingle, blend and develop the way long, slow conventional cooking does. It is important to keep this in mind when preparing soups and stews in particular. Check for seasonings often and adjust them according to your own tastes. If you are making a recipe ahead of time, taste it for seasoning after it has chilled and been reheated; you may find that the flavors are more distinct that they were when you first made it.

Ragout of Beef

Serves 8 **310 calories per serving**

Like all stews, this ragout has a lot of ingredients which are pretty much cooked together at the same time. Make this dish for a small group so that you will have leftovers the next day—stews always taste better the second time around.

2 teaspoons vegetable oil
2 pounds lean, well trimmed round steak, cubed
¾ cup chopped onion
1 small clove garlic, finely chopped
2 cups beef broth
15-ounce can whole tomatoes, drained and chopped
½ cup red wine
2 teaspoons Worcestershire sauce
2 tablespoons flour
1 teaspoon paprika
⅛ teaspoon pepper
4 medium-size potatoes, peeled and diced
1 cup coarsely chopped celery

Put the oil in a 3-quart, microwavable casserole and microwave on High (100 percent) for 1 minute.

Add the meat and onions to the casserole. Microwave on High (100 percent) for 5 to 7 minutes, stirring after 2 minutes. Pour off the fat.

Stir in the broth, tomatoes, wine, Worcestershire sauce, flour, paprika and pepper. Microwave, covered, on Medium (50 percent) for 12 to 15 minutes, until almost tender, stirring every 5 minutes.

Add the potatoes and celery and microwave, covered, on Medium (50 percent) for 18 to 20 minutes, stirring every 5 minutes, until the meat and vegetables are tender.

PROTEIN	25 gm
CARB.	16 gm
FATS	15 gm
CHOL.	80 mg
SODIUM	429 mg

CHAPTER 5

CHICKEN AND OTHER POULTRY

Very few dieters can plan a successful regimen without lots of chicken. Not only is poultry lean and therefore low in calories, but it is endlessly versatile, allowing you to vary your menu so that you can drop pounds without sacrificing interesting meals.

When cooking chicken or other poultry in the microwave, remember to cut the pieces into uniform sizes to promote even cooking. If you are cooking chicken sections in sauce, try to keep them covered with the liquid to prevent any chance of drying.

In some instances, you will want the poultry to look browned. Microwaves do not brown food in the way conventional ovens do and therefore it is necessary to rub the food with a browning agent before cooking. Soy sauce, Kitchen Bouquet sauce, Worcestershire sauce and steak sauce are a few of the recommended agents. You can also brush chicken with melted margarine combined with paprika for an appetizing appearance. Some of the newer ovens have browning elements and there are specially designed browning dishes and utensils which sear and brown food.

Creamy Hungarian Chicken

Serves 4 — **210 calories per serving without noodles**
310 calories per serving with noodles

The browning sauce, combined with the relatively large amount of paprika, gives the chicken pieces a rich appearance. If you are not overly concerned about this, omit the sauce and simply toss the chicken with the oil. (Do not omit the paprika!)

2 whole chicken breasts, boned and skinned
1 teaspoon vegetable oil
¼ teaspoon browning sauce, such as Kitchen Bouquet, soy sauce or Worcestershire
1 cup chopped onion
1 clove garlic, finely chopped
1 teaspoon diet margarine
4 teaspoons paprika
¼ teaspoon cayenne pepper
¼ cup chicken broth
⅛ teaspoon ground black pepper
1 cup plain low-fat yogurt
2 cups cooked egg noodles (optional)

Cut the chicken breasts into 1-inch pieces. Combine the oil and the browning sauce in a bowl. Add the chicken and toss until the pieces are well coated.

Put the onion, garlic and margarine in a 1½-quart microwavable casserole. Microwave on High (100 percent) for 2½ to 3 minutes, stirring once, until the onion is softened.

Sprinkle the chicken with the paprika and cayenne pepper and stir well. Add the chicken and broth to the onion mixture. Cover and microwave on High (100 percent) for 8 minutes, stirring every 2 minutes. Remove the chicken from the sauce, cover and keep warm.

Allow the sauce to cool to lukewarm. Stir in the black pepper and the yogurt.

PROTEIN	29 gm
CARB.	8 gm
FATS	6 gm
CHOL.	76 mg
SODIUM	244 mg

Return the chicken to the sauce in the casserole. Cover and microwave on Medium (50 percent) for 6 to 8 minutes, stirring every 2 minutes, until heated through. Serve over cooked egg noodles.

Honey-Baked Chicken

Serves 4 | **320 calories per serving**

This recipe gives chicken the sweet-sharp flavor so favored in North Africa and the Middle East.

2 tablespoons diet margarine
2 tablespoons flour
¼ cup honey
3 tablespoons coarse-grained mustard
1 teaspoon cinnamon
1 cup plain low-fat yogurt
2 whole chicken breasts, skinned and halved
⅓ cup white wine
Fresh parsley, for garnish

Place the margarine in a 2-cup glass measure and microwave on High (100 percent) for 30 seconds until melted. Stir in the flour. Microwave on High (100 percent) for 15 to 20 seconds, until bubbly. Add the honey, mustard and cinnamon. Let the marinade cool to lukewarm and stir in the yogurt.

Put the chicken in an 8-by-8-inch glass dish. Pour the marinade over, cover and chill for 2 to 3 hours.

Rearrange the chicken pieces so that the meatiest parts are toward the outside of the dish. Pour the wine into the dish. Cover and microwave on Medium (50 percent) for 25 to 30 minutes, rotating the dish a quarter turn every 5 minutes. Uncover and microwave on Medium (50 percent) for 4 to 5 minutes. Garnish with parsley before serving.

Be sure to let each of these sauces reach lukewarm before stirring in the yogurt; otherwise, the yogurt may curdle.

PROTEIN	29 gm
CARB.	27 gm
FATS	9 gm
CHOL.	76 mg
SODIUM	175 mg

Turkey and Corn Stuffed Peppers

Serves 4 **350 calories per serving**

We usually associate ground beef with stuffed peppers, but ground turkey mixed with corn is a delightful and low-fat departure. Stuffed peppers cook so efficiently in the microwave that you will serve them on even the most hurried evening.

4 large green peppers
1 medium-size onion, chopped
1 pound ground turkey
½ cup toasted bread crumbs
8-ounce can whole kernel corn, drained
¼ cup chopped parsley
½ teaspoon dried thyme, crushed
⅛ teaspoon ground black pepper
8-ounce can tomato sauce

Cut the stem, core and seeds out of the peppers and put them in a 9-inch glass pie plate. Cover and microwave on High (100 percent) for 2 minutes. Set aside.

Put the chopped onion in a 1½-quart microwavable casserole. Cover and microwave on High (100 percent) for 2 minutes to soften. Add the ground turkey and microwave, uncovered, on High (100 percent) for 5 minutes, stirring halfway through the cooking time. Drain any fat from the casserole. Add the bread crumbs, corn, 3 tablespoons of parsley, the thyme, pepper, and ½ cup of tomato sauce, and toss to combine.

Spoon the turkey mixture into the green peppers. Spoon the remaining tomato sauce over the top. Microwave on High (100 percent) for 8 minutes, or until the peppers and filling are heated through. Garnish with the remaining parsley before serving.

PROTEIN	27 gm
CARB.	33 gm
FATS	13 gm
CHOL.	1 mg
SODIUM	1619 mg

Pasta Salad with Seasoned Chicken

Serves 6 — **400 calories per serving**

3 cups broccoli florets (about 1 bunch broccoli)
1 tablespoon water
2 whole skinless chicken breasts, halved
1 teaspoon basil
2 teaspoons finely chopped parsley
4 cups cooked pasta spirals or shells
¼ cup low-calorie Italian dressing
1 cup (4 ounces) mozzarella cheese strips
2 cups halved cherry tomatoes
½ cup low-calorie creamy cucumber dressing
1 small red onion, sliced into rings

Put the broccoli and the water in a 9-inch glass pie plate. Cover with transparent wrap, turning back one edge to let the steam escape. Microwave on High (100 percent) for 1½ to 2 minutes, until the broccoli is crisp-tender. Uncover carefully and set the broccoli aside.

Put the chicken in a glass baking dish with the thickest parts at the outside edge. Cover with transparent wrap, turning back one corner to vent. Microwave on High (100 percent) for 8 to 11 minutes, turning the dish every 2 minutes until the flesh is no longer pink and the juices run clear. Let stand for 3 to 4 minutes.

Cut the chicken into ½-inch cubes. Add the basil and parsley and toss.

Combine the pasta and the Italian dressing, toss well and place in a large serving bowl. Top with layers of broccoli, chicken, mozzarella and tomatoes, in that order. Cover with transparent wrap and refrigerate for several hours or overnight.

Just before serving, toss the salad with the cucumber dressing and garnish with red onion rings.

PROTEIN	50 gm
CARB.	49 gm
FATS	24 gm
CHOL.	111 mg
SODIUM	663 mg

Corn-Crisped Chicken

Serves 2 | 310 calories per serving

Everyone has corn flakes in the kitchen cupboard. Crush them for a crispy, crunchy coating for chicken breasts.

¼ cup evaporated skim milk
⅓ cup crushed corn flakes
¼ teaspoon salt
⅛ teaspoon pepper
¼ teaspoon paprika
1 chicken breast, split, rinsed and patted dry

Pour the milk into a shallow dish. Combine the corn flakes, salt, pepper and paprika in another shallow dish. Dip the chicken first in the milk and then in the corn flake mixture to coat.

Arrange the chicken breast in a shallow glass baking dish. Cover with transparent wrap and turn back one corner to vent. Microwave on High (100 percent) for 3 to 6 minutes, rotating the dish a half turn after 2 minutes, until the chicken juices run clear.

PROTEIN	33 gm
CARB.	4 gm
FATS	14 gm
CHOL.	94 mg
SODIUM	518 mg

Turkey Scallops with Marsala Sauce

Serves 4 | 180 calories per serving

Turkey cutlets are very low in fat and their delicate taste blends deliciously with the sweet flavors of Marsala wine and brown sugar. In this recipe, the sauce is thickened at the end of cooking with a little cornstarch.

Increase the cooking time by several minutes to be sure the dish is heated through if it has been stored in the refrigerator, but take care not to overheat as the cornstarch may lose some of its thickening power if it gets too hot.

1 pound turkey breast cutlets, ¼ inch thick
½ cup Marsala wine, dry sherry or vermouth
½ cup chicken broth
2 teaspoons brown sugar
¼ teaspoon salt
¼ teaspoon black pepper
1 teaspoon cornstarch
2 tablespoons water
2 teaspoons grated lemon rind

Put the cutlets in a microwavable baking dish in a single layer. Cover and microwave on Medium (50 percent) for 7 to 9 minutes, turning over and rearranging the cutlets after 4 minutes. Cook until no longer pink. Remove to a platter, cover loosely and keep warm.

Pour the wine and chicken broth into the baking dish. Add the brown sugar, salt and pepper. Microwave on High (100 percent) for 2½ to 3 minutes, until bubbly. Mix the cornstarch with the water to form a smooth paste. Stir the paste into the sauce. Microwave on High (100 percent) for 1½ to 2 minutes, until the sauce is boiling. Add the lemon rind. Adjust the seasonings to taste.

Return the turkey cutlets to the baking dish and spoon the sauce over them. Microwave on High (100 percent) for 1 to 1½ minutes, until heated through.

Thanks to modern shipping and packaging, turkey parts are increasingly available in supermarkets. Turkey breasts are perhaps the most popular item but turkey producers package cutlets, legs and ground turkey, as well.

PROTEIN	28 gm
CARB.	4 gm
FATS	3 gm
CHOL.	79 g
SODIUM	298 mg

CHAPTER 6

FISH AND SEAFOOD

Fish and seafood, being delicate foods, suffer from overcooking—which is why the microwave is the ideal place to cook them. Microwave cooking leaves fish moist and tender and seafood firm and succulent, never soft and mushy. In short, the microwave cooks this fragile food exactly the way a fish lover likes best.

For dieters, fish is ideal: low in fat and calories and high in variety and flavor. Fish is a little more desirable than seafood for people watching their weight and cholesterol, but a little shrimp or a few clams add such zest and excellent flavor to so many dishes, it is a shame not to take advantage of them. Try to use fresh fish whenever possible and do not be afraid to experiment with different kinds. They are all good. Keep a close eye on the fish as it cooks; it is ready when a little pressure from your index finger does not indent it and when it no longer looks translucent.

Fillet of Sole in Lemon Sauce

Serves 4 | **330 calories per serving**

Low in both calories and fat, white-fleshed fish such as sole and flounder are ideal for dieters. You may substitute whatever mild-tasting fish fillets are available in your market, but for the best flavor and texture, try to buy fresh, not frozen, fish.

4 sole fillets (1 to 1½ pounds)
1 tablespoon finely chopped onion
¼ teaspoon white pepper
½ cup white wine
4 teaspoons cornstarch
2 tablespoons lemon juice
1 tablespoon diet margarine
2 tablespoons grated carrot (optional)
2 tablespoons chopped parsley (optional)
2 tablespoons chopped scallion greens (optional)

Put the fish in an 8-by-8-inch microwavable dish so that the thickest portions are at the outside. Sprinkle with the onion and pepper. Pour the wine over the fish. Cover and microwave on High (100 percent) for 5 to 6 minutes, rotating the dish a half turn after 3 minutes.

Mix the cornstarch and the lemon juice to a smooth paste in a 2-cup microwavable measure. Add the liquid from the fish and stir until blended. Add the margarine and microwave on High (100 percent) for 1½ to 2 minutes, until the margarine is melted and the sauce is thickened.

Pour the sauce over the fillets, cover, and microwave on High (100 percent) for 1½ to 2 minutes, until the fish flakes with a fork. Garnish each fillet with carrot, parsley and scallion before serving.

The term "fish" implies the *swimming* creatures of the deep, which have gills and fins. Seafood is everything else: shellfish like clams and oysters, and crustaceans such as lobster, shrimp and crab.

PROTEIN	32 gm
CARB.	5 gm
FATS	5 gm
CHOL.	119 mg
SODIUM	128 mg

Flounder with Vegetables

Serves 4 **180 calories per serving**

A simple and delicately seasoned fish dish—the way most fish ought to be cooked.

1 cup fresh broccoli florets
1 cup fresh cauliflower florets
2 tablespoons water
1 carrot, cut into 2-by-⅛-inch sticks
¼ cup sliced celery, cut on the diagonal
½ teaspoon dried tarragon
1 tablespoon diet margarine
4 6-ounce flounder fillets
2 teaspoons lemon juice
1 tablespoon chopped scallion

Combine the broccoli and cauliflower in a 10-inch microwavable pie dish. Sprinkle with the water and cover with transparent wrap, turning back one corner to release the steam. Microwave on High (100 percent) for 2 minutes.

Add the carrot, celery and tarragon. Dot the vegetables with 1 teaspoon of the margarine. Cover and microwave on High (100 percent) for 2 to 3 minutes, until the vegetables are crisp-tender. Remove them to a serving platter and keep warm.

Place the fish on a pie plate with the thickest portions at the outside. Sprinkle with the lemon juice and scatter the scallion over the top. Dot with the remaining margarine. Cover and microwave on High (100 percent) for 4 to 6 minutes, until the fish flakes with a fork.

Arrange the fish in the center of the serving platter, surrounded by the vegetables.

PROTEIN	53 gm
CARB.	5 gm
FATS	4 gm
CHOL.	153 mg
SODIUM	461 mg

Salmon Steaks with Cucumber Sauce

Serves 4 | **280 calories per serving**

Salmon is a great favorite with most fish lovers, and for good reason. Pairing it with a yogurt-based cucumber sauce is a perfect combination.

¾ cup grated cucumber
1 cup low-fat plain yogurt
1 teaspoon finely chopped scallion
1 teaspoon lemon juice
½ teaspoon salt
½ teaspoon dried dill
¼ teaspoon white pepper
4 6-ounce salmon steaks
1 tablespoon lime juice

To make the sauce, combine the cucumber, yogurt, scallion, lemon juice, salt, dill and pepper. Cover and chill.

Put the salmon steaks in an 8-by-8-inch microwavable dish, with the thickest portions at the outside. Sprinkle with lime juice. Cover with transparent wrap, turning back one corner to let the steam escape. Microwave on High (100 percent) for 8 to 11 minutes, rotating the dish a quarter turn every 2 minutes, until the salmon flakes with a fork.

Remove the skin from the salmon and transfer to a serving platter. Pass the sauce separately.

PROTEIN	36 gm
CARB.	4 gm
FATS	5 gm
CHOL.	67 mg
SODIUM	977 mg

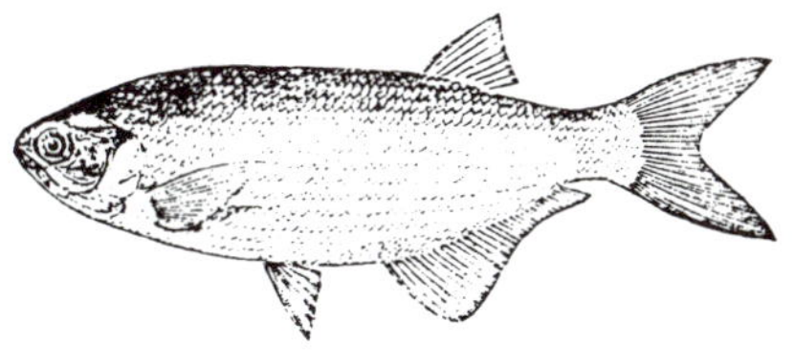

Shrimp-Stuffed Fish Fillets

Serves 6 **295 calories per serving**

For a quietly elegant dish, try these rolled, stuffed fillets. Salad shrimp are the tiny ones.

¼ cup chopped celery
1 tablespoon finely chopped onion
1 teaspoon chopped chives or scallion greens
4 teaspoons diet margarine
6 ounces raw salad shrimp, shelled, deveined and finely chopped
2 tablespoons dry bread crumbs
2 tablespoons lemon juice
¼ teaspoon salt
⅛ teaspoon black pepper
6 4-ounce flounder fillets
1 tablespoon chopped parsley

Put the celery, onion, chives and 1 teaspoon margarine in a 2-cup glass measure. Microwave on High (100 percent) for 1½ minutes until the onion is softened. Stir after 45 seconds. Add the shrimp, bread crumbs, 1 tablespoon of lemon juice, salt and pepper, and stir to combine.

Divide the shrimp mixture among the fillets, placing a mound in the center of each one. Fold the end of each fillet over the filling and secure with a toothpick.

Spray an 8-by-8-inch microwavable dish with vegetable cooking spray. Put the stuffed fillets in the dish and sprinkle with the remaining tablespoon of lemon juice. Dot the fish with the remaining tablespoon of margarine. Cover and microwave on High (100 percent) for 6 to 8 minutes, rotating the dish a half turn after 3 minutes, until the fish can be flaked with a fork. Allow to stand, covered, for 3 to 4 minutes. Garnish with chopped parsley before serving.

PROTEIN	62 gm
CARB.	3 gm
FATS	18 gm
CHOL.	206 mg
SODIUM	669 mg

Shrimp and Vegetable Scampi

Serves 4 | **250 calories per serving**

Marinate the shrimp for at least 30 minutes; the acid in the lemon juice will partially "cook" the shellfish even before microwaving.

3 tablespoons diet margarine, melted
¼ teaspoon grated lemon rind
Juice of ½ lemon
3 cloves garlic, finely chopped
½ teaspoon dried thyme
1 pound raw shrimp, shelled and deveined
2 medium-size carrots, cut into 2-by-⅛-inch sticks (about 2 cups)
1 tablespoon water
¼ pound snow pea pods, trimmed
¼ cup bamboo shoots, drained
¼ cup sliced water chestnuts, drained

Combine the margarine, lemon rind and juice, garlic and thyme in a large shallow bowl. Add the shrimp and stir to coat. Cover and chill for 30 minutes.

Arrange the carrot sticks around the edge of a microwavable 10-inch pie plate. Sprinkle with water and cover with transparent wrap, turning back one edge to vent. Microwave on High (100 percent) for 2 minutes. Remove the wrap and drain off the liquid.

Place the pea pods, bamboo shoots and water chestnuts on top of the carrots, also in a circle. Top with the marinated shrimp. Cover and microwave on High (100 percent) for 4 to 6 minutes, rotating the dish a half turn after 2 minutes. Remove the cover and rearrange the shrimp. Cover and microwave on High (100 percent) for 1 to 2 minutes, until the shrimp are cooked.

PROTEIN	29 gm
CARB.	10 gm
FATS	2 gm
CHOL.	142 mg
SODIUM	246 mg

Red Clam Sauce for Linguine

Serves 4 **230 calories per serving**

Italian cooks have known for ages that adding fresh clams to a simple red sauce converts a pasta meal into a special event filled with robust flavor. Using a microwave to open the clams and cook the sauce makes it easy and fast.

2 dozen fresh clams, scrubbed
½ cup chopped onion
1 clove garlic, finely chopped
1 tablespoon olive oil
15-ounce can whole tomatoes, chopped and juice reserved
½ teaspoon dried oregano
Salt and pepper
2 tablespoons chopped parsley
2 cups hot cooked linguine

Arrange the clams in a 10- or 12-inch microwavable dish in a single layer. Cover loosely with transparent wrap and microwave on High (100 percent) 2 to 3 minutes, just until the clams pop open. Set them aside.

Put the onion, garlic and oil in a 1½-quart microwavable casserole. Microwave on High (100 percent) for 1½ to 2 minutes until the onion is softened.

Drain any liquid from the clams into the casserole and stir in the tomatoes and juice, oregano and salt and pepper to taste. Microwave, uncovered, on High (100 percent) for 5 to 6 minutes. Transfer the mixture to a food processor or blender and puree.

Return the puree to the casserole. Remove the clams from their shells and stir into the sauce. Add the parsley. Microwave, uncovered, on High (100 percent) for 3 to 5 minutes to heat through. Serve over linguine.

PROTEIN	5 gm
CARB.	18 gm
FATS	1 gm
CHOL.	62 mg
SODIUM	725 mg

Chilled Manicotti Stuffed with Tuna

Serves 6 **120 calories per serving**

This is a pretty dish to serve in warm weather or whenever you cannot easily find fresh or frozen fish. The flavorful stuffed pasta can be made well in advance of the meal—toss a green salad and you are all set!

½ pound fresh spinach, washed and trimmed
6½-ounce can tuna in water, drained
⅔ cup peeled, chopped cucumber
¼ cup chopped celery
2 tablespoons diced onion
3 tablespoons olive oil
3 tablespoons red wine vinegar
1 tablespoon sugar
1 small clove garlic, finely chopped
Salt and pepper
6 manicotti pasta tubes, cooked al dente and cooled
½ cup low-fat plain yogurt

Soak the spinach in cold water and then rinse well. Shake off the water but do not dry. Put the spinach in a 1½-quart microwavable casserole. Cover and microwave on High (100 percent) for 3 to 4 minutes until the spinach is tender, stirring after 2 minutes. Drain, pressing out the excess water.

Add the tuna, cucumber, celery and onion to the spinach and chill.

Combine the oil, vinegar, sugar, garlic and salt and pepper to taste. Pour the mixture over the chilled spinach mixture and toss until evenly coated.

Carefully spoon the mixture into the pasta tubes. Arrange them on a serving plate, cover and chill. Top each tube with a spoonful of yogurt before serving.

PROTEIN	11 gm
CARB.	15 gm
FATS	1 gm
CHOL.	22 mg
SODIUM	483 mg

CHAPTER 7

BEEF, PORK AND LAMB

Red meat rounds out anyone's diet—whether it is a reducing one or simply a healthy one—and provides a range of wonderful, bold flavors. While nearly everyone is aware that too much red meat is not good for us, in moderation it provides excellent protein, iron and many other nutrients.

There are almost as many cuts of meat as there are ways of cooking them. The less expensive cuts generally require a bit more seasoning and longer cooking. With the microwave, this is measured in minutes, not hours. Flank steak and round, for instance, can be cooked so that they are every bit as appetizing and appealing as sirloin. Just try to buy meat with as little fat as possible and trim away any excess before you begin to cook what you have chosen.

Beef Stroganoff

Serves 6 | **365 calories per serving**

When a recipe calls for a browning and seasoning sauce, such as this one does, you have a choice. You can add a little Kitchen Bouquet, which will give you color but little flavor, or you can add an ingredient such as steak sauce, teriyaki sauce, Worcestershire sauce or soy sauce, all of which will provide color and distinct flavor.

1 pound beef sirloin steak
2 tablespoon white wine or dry vermouth
2 teaspoons dried tarragon
2 teaspoons vegetable oil
½ teaspoon browning and seasoning sauce
1 medium-size onion, thinly sliced
1 pound sliced mushrooms, trimmed and sliced
¼ cup plain low-fat yogurt
2 tablespoons flour
⅛ teaspoon pepper
¼ cup beef broth, at room temperature
4½ cups freshly cooked egg noodles

Trim all the fat from the meat. Cut the trimmed meat into 3-inch strips, about ⅛ inch thick. Put the strips in an 8-by-11½-inch microwavable baking dish. Add the wine, tarragon, oil and browning sauce and stir until the meat is well coated. Marinate for 20 minutes at room temperature.

Add the onion and mushrooms to the meat and cover and microwave on Medium (50 percent) for 8 to 10 minutes, stirring every 3 minutes.

Mix together the yogurt, flour, pepper, and beef broth. Pour the yogurt mixture over the meat and stir. Cover and microwave on High (100 percent) for 5 to 7 minutes, stirring every 2 minutes, until the sauce is thickened and simmering. Serve over the noodles.

PROTEIN	19 gm
CARB.	7 gm
FATS	28 gm
CHOL.	71 mg
SODIUM	102 mg

Spicy Beef Barbecue

Serves 4 — 330 calories per serving

These hearty sandwiches hit the spot on cold winter afternoons—a tasty departure from the more familiar sorts of roast beef sandwiches.

8-ounce can tomato sauce
1 medium-size onion, finely chopped
1 clove garlic, finely chopped
2 tablespoons cider vinegar
1 teaspoon dried mustard
1 teaspoon paprika
4–5 drops hot pepper sauce
1 pound cooked roast beef, thinly sliced
4 slices thin-sliced bread

Combine the tomato sauce, onion, garlic, vinegar, mustard, paprika and hot pepper sauce in a 4-cup glass measure. Cover and microwave on High (100 percent) for 5 to 6 minutes, stirring after 3 minutes.

Put the beef in an 8-by-8-inch microwavable dish. Pour the sauce over the meat, stirring to distribute. Cover and microwave on High (100 percent) for 3 to 5 minutes, until heated through. Serve the barbecued beef on the bread slices.

PROTEIN	36 gm
CARB.	15 gm
FATS	13 gm
CHOL.	80 mg
SODIUM	572 mg

Lamb Chops and Mustard Sauce

Serves 4 — 340 calories per serving

Who can resist lamb chops? Let them marinate for a half hour with spicy mustard and a little vermouth and they are better than ever.

¼ cup Dijon mustard
2 tablespoons vegetable oil
¼ cup dry vermouth
¼ teaspoon pepper
4 lamb chops, about ¾ inch thick

Combine the mustard, oil, vermouth and pepper to make the marinade.

Put the lamb chops in a glass or porcelain dish. Pour the marinade over the chops, cover and chill for 30 minutes.

Heat a microwave browning dish for 5 to 7 minutes on High (100 percent). Lift the lamb chops from the marinade and pat them dry with paper towels. Put them in the browning dish and microwave on High (100 percent) for 1 minute. Turn the chops over and microwave on High (100 percent) for 2 to 3 minutes, depending on the degree of doneness you prefer. To prevent over-browning, remove the chops from the dish as soon as they are done.

PROTEIN	16 gm
CARB.	1 gm
FATS	29 gm
CHOL.	46 mg
SODIUM	222 mg

BROWNING DISHES

With so many cooks using microwaves for nearly all their cooking, it is not surprising that manufacturers have come out with a line of microwavable containers that promote browning. These grills and pans are specially coated with a material that absorbs microwave energy. The hot surface causes the outside of any food touching it to sear and brown. Uncoated portions stay cool and most of the products are designed with feet to lift them off countertops.

These pans cannot be used on conventional stoves or in conventional ovens. They have to be heated in the microwave first, without food, for several minutes to insure that the coated surface gets sufficiently hot. Never use vegetable sprays, or line them with paper towels or plastic. They get so hot that the oil could spatter and the paper or plastic ignite. Before using browning pans, be sure the oven cavity is clean and grease-free.

Texas-Style Chili

Serves 6 **350 calories per serving**

The wonderful thing about chili is how truly easy it is to make. And it tastes so good, too! Some Texans might prefer a hotter version of the stew, but for most tenderfoots, this is just about right. However, fiddle with the seasonings after you have made this chili once and adjust it to your own particular taste.

1½ pounds boneless stewing beef, cut into ½-inch cubes and well trimmed
6-ounce can tomato paste
1 cup chopped onion
½ cup chopped green pepper
16-ounce can whole tomatoes, chopped, with juices
1½ cups beef broth
1 tablespoon chili powder
2 small cloves garlic, finely chopped
1 teaspoon dried oregano
1 teaspoon sugar
½ teaspoon ground cumin

Combine all the ingredients in a 3-quart microwavable casserole, stirring to mix well. Cover and microwave on High (100 percent) for 5 minutes. Stir well.

Microwave, covered, on Medium (50 percent) for 50 to 60 minutes, stirring every 10 minutes, until the meat is fork-tender. Allow to stand, covered, for 10 minutes before serving.

PROTEIN	24 gm
CARB.	12 gm
FATS	23 gm
CHOL.	79 mg
SODIUM	827 mg

Peppered Pork Chops

Serves 4 | 380 calories per serving

Coriander seeds, available in supermarkets in the spice section, will give these chops a jolt of flavor. If you want a slightly milder dish—but one that still has the full flavors of garlic and crushed peppercorns, omit the seeds altogether.

3 tablespoons soy sauce
1 tablespoon crushed coriander seeds
2 cloves garlic, crushed
8 crushed peppercorns
1 teaspoon brown sugar
3 tablespoons soy sauce
4 pork loin chops, about 1 inch thick
1 tablespoon vegetable oil

Combine the soy sauce, coriander, garlic, peppercorns and brown sugar and mix well. Put the chops in a glass or porcelain dish and pour the marinade over them. Cover and chill for 30 to 60 minutes. Brush the chops occasionally with the marinade.

Heat a browning dish on High (100 percent) for 5 minutes. Pat the chops dry with paper towels.

Add the oil to the browning dish and tilt the pan to coat the bottom. Put the chops in the dish and microwave on High (100 percent) for 1 minute. Turn the chops over and microwave on High (100 percent) for 1 minute more.

Arrange the chops with the meatiest part toward the edge of the dish. Cover and microwave on Medium (50 percent) for 6 minutes. Turn the chops over, cover them again, and microwave on Medium (50 percent) for 6 to 7 minutes more, until the meat near the bone is no longer pink.

PROTEIN	23 gm
CARB.	2 gm
FATS	31 gm
CHOL.	87 mg
SODIUM	890 mg

Marinated Flank Steak

Serves 4 **230 calories per serving**

Flank steak has to be one of the best beef buys available. When properly marinated, which tenderizes, it tastes as good as the best sirloin, yet is lower in fat. Be sure to carve this cut of meat against, or across, the grain into thin slices.

½ cup fresh orange juice
¼ cup red wine vinegar
3 tablespoons soy sauce
1 tablespoon honey
¼ teaspoon pepper
1 tablespoon vegetable oil
1 pound flank steak

Combine the orange juice, vinegar, soy sauce, honey, pepper and oil in an 8-by-8-inch glass baking dish.

Score both sides of the steak with several diagonal cuts. Put the steak in the marinade. Spoon the marinade over the steak and chill for 6 hours or overnight, turning occasionally.

Heat a microwave browning dish on High (100 percent) for 5 to 6 minutes.

Remove the meat from the marinade, pat dry with paper towels and put it on the browning dish. Microwave on High (100 percent) for 2 to 3 minutes on each side. Let stand 2 minutes. Cut the steak across the grain into thin slices and serve.

PROTEIN	25 gm
CARB.	9 gm
FATS	10 gm
CHOL.	79 mg
SODIUM	906 mg

Spaghetti Sauce

Serves 6 | **260 calories per serving without spaghetti**
360 calories per serving with spaghetti

Convenient as it is to make spaghetti sauce in a microwave, you will have to taste it for seasoning and, if necessary, add more than the amounts indicated in the recipe. Spoon the sauce over cooked spaghetti, linguine or fettuccine.

1 pound lean ground beef
1 medium-size onion, chopped
2 cloves garlic, finely chopped
28-ounce can whole tomatoes, with juice
¾ cup beef broth or dry red wine
6-ounce can tomato paste
¼ cup chopped parsley
2 teaspoons dried oregano
1 teaspoon dried basil
Freshly ground pepper
½ teaspoon salt
3 cups freshly cooked spaghetti (optional)

Put the beef, onion and garlic in a 2-quart microwavable casserole and stir to combine. Microwave on High (100 percent) for 5 to 6 minutes, stirring after 2 minutes, until the meat is browned. Drain off the fat.

Puree the tomatoes in a blender or food processor. Add the pureed tomatoes to the meat. Stir in the broth or wine, tomato paste, parsley, oregano, basil, salt and pepper to taste. Cover and microwave on High (100 percent) for 10 minutes, stirring after 5 minutes. Taste for seasoning and adjust if necessary. Microwave, uncovered, on High (100 percent) for 10 to 12 minutes more to develop the flavors.

PROTEIN	16 gm
CARB.	13 gm
FATS	16 gm
CHOL.	51 mg
SODIUM	429 mg

CHAPTER 8

DESSERTS

Desserts are the crowning glory of any meal and even when you are watching calories, you can still look forward to a sweet, indulgent finale. Not surprisingly, fresh and frozen fruit are dominant ingredients in most "diet" desserts. They are full of flavor and sweetness, yet are quite low in calories and have no fat.

Use fruits when they are in season and ripe, bursting with all their natural flavor—as well as easy to find and attractively priced. In most of these recipes the fruit itself sweetens the dessert with only a little additional sugar or honey.

Using a microwave to prepare these desserts adds to their appeal. The fruit maintains its texture and shape and takes only minutes to poach or soften enough to blend with the other flavors in the dessert.

LABEL LOGIC

If you are using frozen or canned fruit, read the label carefully to check for added sugar. Many fruits are packed in sugar syrup and they are high in calories. Look for products packed without sugar or in "light" syrups and natural juices.

Tropical Bananas

Serves 6 **90 calories per serving**

Green-tipped bananas are not as ripe as those that are completely yellow and will hold up better to cooking. If the bananas are green further down than their tips, let them ripen for another day or two before using.

8-ounce can unsweetened, crushed pineapple
1 teaspoon honey
2 teaspoons cornstarch
2 tablespoons water
3 large, green-tipped bananas
1 tablespoon lemon juice
2 tablespoons chopped pecans

Drain the pineapple, reserving the juice.

Combine the pineapple juice and the honey in a 1-cup glass measure. Microwave on High (100 percent) for 1 minute or until boiling.

Combine the cornstarch with the water and stir until smooth. Add to the juice mixture and stir to blend. Microwave on High (100 percent) for 1 to 1½ minutes, until the sauce thickens.

Peel the bananas and cut them in half lengthwise. Brush with lemon juice.

Place the bananas, cut side up, in an 8-by-8-inch microwavable dish. Microwave on Medium (50 percent) for 3 minutes, rotating the pan a half turn after 2 minutes.

Pour the sauce over the bananas. Top with the crushed pineapple and chopped pecans. Microwave on Medium (50 percent) for 1 to 1½ minutes until they reach the consistency you like.

PROTEIN	1 gm
CARB.	19 gm
FATS	2 gm
CHOL.	0 mg
SODIUM	1 mg

Poached Pears with Peach Sauce

Serves 8 **90 calories per serving**

Pears are one of the best fruits to poach—they retain their firm texture and absorb the flavor of the poaching liquid without losing their own unique taste.

4 large ripe Anjou or Bosc pears
2½ cups low-calorie cranberry juice
2 teaspoons vanilla extract
1 pound ripe peaches, peeled and pitted or 12-ounce package quick-frozen sliced peaches, defrosted
½ teaspoon almond extract
Fresh mint for decoration (optional)

Peel, halve and core the pears. Place them in an 8-by-8-inch microwavable dish, cut side up.

Combine the cranberry juice with the vanilla and pour over the pears. Cover with transparent wrap, turning back one corner to vent. Microwave on High (100 percent) for 8 to 10 minutes, rotating the dish a half turn every 4 minutes, until the pears are just tender. Let stand, covered, for 2 minutes.

Drain the pears, reserving the liquid. Cover and refrigerate until well chilled.

Combine the peaches with the almond extract and ¼ cup of the reserved poaching liquid in a food processor or blender and puree. Chill the puree for at least 1 hour.

To serve, place 1 pear half on each dessert plate. Top with the cold peach sauce and decorate with fresh mint.

PROTEIN	1 gm
CARB.	22 gm
FATS	0 gm
CHOL.	0 mg
SODIUM	6 mg

Baked Granola Apples

Serves 4 | **120 calories per serving**

Quick and oh-so-easy, these baked apples are just right for chilly autumn days. Buy firm, tart apples such as Granny Smiths, Romes or Jonathans.

2 large baking apples
2 tablespoons lemon juice
4 teaspoons diet margarine
4 teaspoons packed brown sugar
4 tablespoons granola cereal, slightly crushed

Cut the apples in half through the stem and remove the cores. Place them, cut side up, in an 8-by-8-inch microwavable baking dish. Sprinkle with lemon juice.

Top each apple half with 1 teaspoon of margarine and 1 teaspoon of brown sugar. Cover the dish with transparent wrap, turning back one corner to vent. Microwave on High (100 percent) for 4 to 6 minutes, rotating the dish a half turn after 2 minutes, until the apples are tender.

Sprinkle each half with 1 tablespoon of granola. Cover and microwave on High for 1 to 1½ minutes. Let the apples stand for 2 minutes before serving.

PROTEIN	1 gm
CARB.	20 gm
FATS	5 gm
CHOL.	0 mg
SODIUM	63 mg

POACHING MAGIC

Poaching fruit in a microwave is simple and quick. There is no need to wait for the poaching liquid to come to a simmer, nor do you have to watch closely to be sure it does not boil. Just put the fruit and poaching liquid in a pan and microwave on High (100 percent) for 10 minutes or less, according to the specific recipe.

Lemon Yogurt Pie

Serves 6 (makes one 8-inch pie) **210 calories per serving**

This chilled pie might be called a "mock" lemon chiffon pie. Its rich, creamy taste will satisfy your sweetest dessert craving.

3 tablespoons diet margarine
1 ⅓ cups finely crushed granola cereal
1 tablespoon (1 package) unflavored gelatin
6 tablespoons sugar
¼ teaspoon salt
2 large eggs, separated
1 cup water
1 cup low-fat lemon yogurt
Grated rind of ¼ lemon

To make the crust, put the margarine in a medium-size glass dish and microwave on High (100 percent) for 30 seconds. Add the granola and mix well.

Spray an 8-inch microwavable pie plate with vegetable cooking spray. Press the granola mixture onto the bottom and sides of the plate. Microwave on High (100 percent) for 1 to 2 minutes, turning once during baking. Set aside to cool.

To make the filling, combine the gelatin, 4 tablespoons of sugar and the salt in a 4-cup glass measure and stir until thoroughly mixed.

Beat the egg yolks with the water and stir into the gelatin mixture. Microwave on High (100 percent) for 2½ to 3 minutes, stirring every 30 seconds, until the mixture starts to come to the boil. Chill, stirring occasionally, until the mixture mounds slightly when dropped from a spoon. This will take about 20 minutes but watch it carefully. Do not let it set too firm.

Beat the egg whites with an electric mixer at medium speed until foamy. Increase the speed to high and grad-

In many microwave recipes that call for gelatin, the powder need not be softened first in liquid and then dissolved. Simply combine the dry granules with the dry and liquid ingredients and microwave on High (100 percent) for a few minutes, or less. Read the recipe carefully, though, to be sure this is appropriate.

PROTEIN	8 gm
CARB.	26 gm
FATS	10 gm
CHOL.	64 mg
SODIUM	197 mg

ually add the remaining 2 tablespoons of sugar. Continue to beat until stiff peaks form.

Fold the yogurt into the chilled gelatin mixture. Fold the beaten egg whites into the yogurt mixture and mound into the prepared crust. Smooth the top and chill for 3 to 4 hours, or until firm. Sprinkle with grated lemon rind before serving.

Vanilla Custard

Serves 2 | **100 calories per serving**

Who said custard had to be fattening? This one is low in calories and takes only minutes to prepare. Cooking custard in the microwave eliminates the need for constant stirring, yet produces an exquisitely silky texture.

1 cup skim milk
1 large egg
2 teaspoons sugar
½ teaspoon vanilla extract
⅛ teaspoon cinnamon
⅛ teaspoon salt

Pour the milk into a glass measure. Microwave on High (100 percent) for 2 to 3 minutes to scald. Do not allow the milk to boil.

Beat the egg in a small bowl. Add the sugar, vanilla, cinnamon and salt and blend well.

Gradually stir the hot milk into the egg mixture. Pour into 2 glass custard cups and microwave on Medium (50 percent) for 5 to 6 minutes, rotating each dish a half turn after 3 minutes, until the custard is just set and a knife inserted near the edge of the cup comes out clean. Allow to stand for 30 minutes. Serve warm or chilled.

PROTEIN	8 gm
CARB.	11 gm
FATS	3 gm
CHOL.	128 mg
SODIUM	240 mg

Pumpkin Mousse

Serves 8 **130 calories per serving**

Light, smooth and nicely flavored with ginger and orange, this dessert is fancy enough for company and easy enough to make for every day. Take care not to chill the mousse longer than recommended; it should be firm, but not *too* firm.

1 tablespoon (1 package) unflavored gelatin
½ cup packed brown sugar
½ teaspoon cinnamon
16-ounce can pureed pumpkin
½ cup skim milk
¼ teaspoon vanilla extract
3 large eggs, separated
1 teaspoon finely chopped crystallized ginger
2 teaspoons grated orange rind
1 large egg white
2 tablespoons sugar

Combine the gelatin, brown sugar and cinnamon in a large bowl. Add the pumpkin, milk and vanilla and stir well. Microwave on High (100 percent) for 3 to 3½ minutes, stirring every 30 seconds, until the mixture starts to come to the boil.

Beat the 3 egg yolks in a small bowl. Add ½ cup of the hot pumpkin mixture to the egg yolks and stir to blend. Stir this mixture back into the pumpkin in the large bowl. Microwave on High (100 percent) for 45 seconds. Stir in the ginger and the orange rind.

Put the bowl in a pan of ice water or chill it in the refrigerator. Stir occasionally until the mixture mounds slightly when dropped from a spoon. This will take about 20 minutes but should be watched carefully. Do not let it get too firm.

Beat the 4 egg whites with an electric mixer at me-

PROTEIN	7 gm
CARB.	22 gm
FATS	2 gm
CHOL.	95 mg
SODIUM	44 mg

dium speed until foamy. Increase the speed to high and gradually add the sugar. Continue beating until stiff peaks form.

Fold the meringue into the chilled pumpkin mixture. Spoon into 8 dessert glasses or dishes. Chill, covered, for 2 to 3 hours.

Apple Bake Supreme

Serves 4 to 6 — **70 calories per serving**

Creamy and cinnamon-scented, this apple dessert even has a tantalizing hint of vanilla.

2 large Granny Smith apples, peeled, cored, cut in half crosswise and thinly sliced
2 tablespoons water
2 tablespoons lemon juice
1 tablespoon sugar
½ teaspoon cinnamon
4 tablespoons (2 ounces) low-calorie cream cheese
2 teaspoons skim milk
¼ teaspoon vanilla extract
2 tablespoons chopped pecans

Place the apple slices in a 2-quart microwavable casserole and sprinkle with the water and lemon juice.

Combine the sugar and cinnamon and toss with the apples. Cover and microwave on High (100 percent) for 4 to 6 minutes, stirring once, until the apples are tender.

Combine the cream cheese, skim milk and vanilla in a small microwavable dish, stirring until blended. Microwave on High (100 percent) for 20 to 30 seconds, until warm.

Spoon the cream cheese mixture over the apples. Sprinkle with the chopped pecans and serve at once.

PROTEIN	1 gm
CARB.	10 gm
FATS	4 gm
CHOL.	5 mg
SODIUM	29 mg

Frozen Blueberry Clouds

Serves 6 | 100 calories per serving

This pudding, lightened with egg whites and then frozen, is sure to please even the most ardent ice cream lover in the family.

1½ cups fresh blueberries or 12-ounce package frozen blueberries, thawed
8 teaspoons sugar
4 teaspoons cornstarch
¾ cup plain low-fat yogurt
1 teaspoon vanilla extract
1 large egg white
¼ teaspoon cream of tartar

Drain the fruit, if frozen, and reserve the liquid. Sprinkle with 6 teaspoons of sugar. Set aside 1 cup of water or add enough water to the drained liquid to make 1 cup.

Combine the cornstarch and the remaining 2 teaspoons of sugar in a 1-quart microwavable casserole. Gradually add the water or blueberry liquid, stirring until the mixture is smooth. Microwave on High (100 percent) for 2½ to 3 minutes, stirring after 1½ minutes, until the mixture is thickened and bubbly. Let cool.

Set aside ¼ cup of blueberries for decoration. Combine the remaining blueberries with the cornstarch mixture, yogurt and vanilla.

Beat the egg white with the cream of tartar until stiff peaks form. Fold in the fruit mixture. Cover with transparent wrap and freeze until firm.

To serve, cut into 6 servings and top each with the reserved blueberries.

PROTEIN	1 gm
CARB.	13 gm
FATS	1 gm
CHOL.	4 mg
SODIUM	55 mg

INDEX